Working Capital

It Takes More Than Money

Vol. 1

Sean K. Murphy

Published by SKMurphy, 2020.

WORKING CAPITAL
First edition. November 23, 2020.
Copyright © 2020 Sean K. Murphy
Editor: Gabriela Joseph

ISBNs

978-1-954279-00-1 - EPUB
978-1-954279-01-8 - MOBI
978-1-954279-02-5 - PDF
978-1-954279-03-2 - Paperback
978-1-954279-04-9 - Audiobook

SKMurphy, Inc.
San Jose, CA

This book is dedicated to all of the entrepreneurs I have had the privilege of getting to know at Bootstrappers Breakfast meetings over the last fourteen years. I am grateful for all that I have learned from you. And I have taken the liberty of using your questions, problems, and suggestions as key contributions to this book.

Contents

Introduction

The truth is that there is no one way to succeed. Despite the plethora of startups and entrepreneurs in Silicon Valley, there is no paved road, no such thing as a safe venture. Instead, there are a fundamental set of constraints specific to each business. The tactics and resources that make a lawn mowing service successful, for example, look significantly different from a Tesla dealership or an offshore software consulting firm. Startup literature is brimming with funding guides and networking schemes. But unless you know how to leverage the working capital and assets specific to your business, those how-to books won't make a difference.

I visualize these three types of working capital as three legs of a stool. Intellectual, social, and financial capital each provide an important but distinct kind of support for your business. And like a stool, the seat is only stable once all three legs are in balance. But a startup's self-assembly is more complicated than crafting a stool. For instance, there is no warehouse of spare stool legs to attach. Entrepreneurs must grow their wooden legs, building all three aspects of their business in parallel. Feel free to choose which capital to start with, but keep in mind that if you place too much effort on any one "leg," the startup becomes less viable.

Instead of fixating on a narrow path to success, I want to provide a bootstrapper's narrative to starting your own business with these three perspectives at the forefront, offering both conceptual and practical advice for how to best leverage your financial, intellectual, and social capital. Here, the key is understanding the parameters of your idea, reaching out to prospects early, failing often, and to not being afraid of detours.

This book is the first of an ongoing series about entrepreneurship and startup creation. Email skmurphy@skmurphy.com for updates on revisions and new releases, and to receive free supplemental worksheets and tools.

Overview
What You Need to Start a Business

*"How are you supposed to have a startup in a garage
if the garage costs millions of dollars?"*
Ajay Royan (quoted in The Economist)

The standard definition of working capital is as a purely financial resource. That definition is too narrow and paints an inaccurate picture of what's really needed to craft, explore, and market your idea.

Spoiler Alert: It takes financial, intellectual, and social capital to start a business.

Financial Capital

Starting a new business does require some initial money, whether for office space, permits, licenses, inventory, product development, manufacturing, or marketing.

As a startup, you might have "real" or financial assets in the following categories:

- Bank accounts
- Equipment and tools
- Real property (i.e. office building, automobiles, furniture)
- Inventory and physical work in progress
- Accounts Receivable–including recurring revenue obligations

Startup capital is also referred to as "seed money." Here are some typical sources:

- Bootstrapping
- Consulting / Freelancing / Day job

- VC funding
- Crowdfunding

Intellectual Capital

Intellectual capital refers to business assets that demonstrate your business value. They are your know-how or "have done, can do" at both an individual and a team level. This is not just a recipe, but a recipe that you or your team have delivered on in the past. This know-how is typically presented to customers as past accomplishments that are indicative of future performance. These include:

- Patents, trademarks and trade secrets (i.e. "classic" intellectual property)
- Copyrighted content
- Skills or expertise demonstrated in practice at an individual or team level
- Degrees, certifications, and externally recognized expertise (that influence prospect or customer purchase decisions) and capabilities (what customers either require as a minimum to consider you or help to differentiate your startup can also be included).
- Templates, checklists, and other process and diagnostic criteria--these may be disclosed to prospects, customers, or partners, or they may be treated as trade secrets.

Social Capital

Finally, there is the firm's social capital. This is the set of business relationships that have been established with customers, partners, suppliers, and prospects. These business relationships enable access to domain experts, introductions to potential cofounders and early employees, and conversations with prospects who may become early customers.

It's as much about **who you know** as it is **how you know them**. These contacts could come from:

- Family, friends, and acquaintances
- The firm's current suppliers, partners, customers, and advisors
- Co-workers, customers, and suppliers from prior employment
- Alumni: classmates and teachers from high school, college, and university
- Industry, professional, or association memberships
- Permission to contact lists (e.g., mailing lists)

Summary

This overview was meant to help orient the beginning entrepreneur within the realm of working capital. The goal now is to delve into more detail about the particular properties and unique aspects of these three flavors of capital, starting with everyone's favorite—financial capital.

Financial Capital
A practical introduction to calculating costs and
funding your startup

"Everybody needs money. That's why they call it money."
David Mamet in the movie "Heist"
(voiced by Danny DeVito playing bad guy Mickey Bergman)

Mamet's dialog underlines a fundamental truth: people understand
the value of money. We know that sound financial capital opens a lot
of doors and provides entrepreneurs with access to vital resources.
Starting a new business does require some initial money, whether for
office space, permits, licenses, inventory, product development,
manufacturing, or marketing.

Probably you'll have financial capital as one or more of the following
categories:

- Bank accounts
- Equipment and tools
- Real property (i.e. office building, automobiles, furniture)
- Inventory and physical work in progress
- Accounts Receivable–including recurring revenue obligations

We know it's essential to make money. We know that money matters.
And there are countless sources and self-help books focused on
raising money to produce a venture-backed startup. This chapter is
not one of them.

Instead, my goal is to equip entrepreneurs with the necessary
knowledge to calculate how much investment is needed—from
exploring an idea to building traction and scaling up—and to provide
essential funding options and methods for shortening time to
revenue.

Calculating How Much Money You Need

Every phase of the startup process—from exploring the idea, to building traction, to establishing a niche and scaling up—has different goals and priorities. And no two startups are exactly alike. To ensure your investments provide value, plan to meet your objectives during every phase and avoid spending money where there is no clear route to revenue.

Here are different types of expenses categories to consider during the idea/formation and early market exploration phase:

- Formation:
    - Incorporation
    - Legal Fees for software, license, contract review
    - Business License and other permits
- Operating Expenses:
    - Accounting Fees
    - Co-working facility and/or meeting room rental
    - Engineering tools and subscriptions
- Outreach Expenses:
    - Conferences and major events
    - Organization membership (professional, industry, networking) and local event fees
    - Basic listing fees in directories
    - Basic advertising (e.g. adwords)
    - Website creation and maintenance
    - Travel, meals and entertainment for sales calls

Exploration

Your exploration phase may last anywhere from a few weeks to a few months. During this stage, you're spending roughly one quarter of your time and are still very much dependent on a full-time day job. This is when you conduct interviews and talk to potential prospects.

Most of your expenses at this stage should be directed at creating those conversations (e.g. group membership fees or networking event attendance fees). You might also look into creating a website or blog to help gauge customer interest but avoid spending too much on development until you're certain there's a need for your product or service.

When assessing desirability, I suggest you price low enough to be credible given the application area (no one wants to buy a car for $10), but not so high that it would turn anyone off. If people are not willing to pay even at a low price, then you have a problem. Pro tip: free is not a price.

The most common startup failure story is building what customers asked for, but never paid for. The startup is left with products that people decided, in the end, not to buy. It's then back to square one, spending more time and money on an extended exploration period.

To avoid that, here are two methods of shortening time to successful offers:

1. **Adjust your beliefs based on new information** - The technical term for this is "Bayesian updating." Essentially, it means that you don't treat your hypotheses as true or false but as a likelihood or probability estimate. With new information, you adjust the likelihood based on supporting or disconfirming evidence. Start by establishing a consensus estimate with your team and make some predictions: "If we talk to X people who fit our customer profile, we anticipate that at least Y% will express interest (or have this problem)". Mark Zimmerman advises that "Beliefs are knobs, not switches!" The natural human tendency is to imagine that beliefs are true or false but there are degrees of certainty, odds, and likelihoods. With new evidence it's vital to update beliefs rather than throw them away.

2. **Build on past accomplishments** - Write up your company's origin story, and describe where you've encountered the problem in the past. This exercise is meant to help you articulate the solution and define potential prospects. Your previous case studies can also act as a baseline for your Bayesian updating.

It can be difficult to estimate how long your exploration efforts will take in order to converge on a particular customer-need-solution trifecta. It's common to go through several iterations. As a rule of thumb, if you cannot find interest after a dozen to two dozen interviews, you should make a significant adjustment to one or more of your hypotheses. And as with any debugging effort, it's always useful to have multiple hypotheses you can explore in parallel and it's better if you only change one aspect of your business at a time (e.g. same customer different problem or different customer same problem).

Building

If you are going to complete a transaction, then the ***appearance*** of a viable business (e.g. a nice website and social media presence) is no longer sufficient. A software business will need a real software license agreement and a hardware product will require all of the expenses associated with building a working prototype and securing the appropriate permits, licenses, and legal structure will incur some additional costs.

Once you've developed your business idea and generated some interest, the real problem becomes figuring out who will pay. You are fairly certain there's a market and are now fine-tuning your pitch and debugging the sales process. From a software or service perspective, this might be when you consider adding features to secure a deal. This might also be when you start spending money to advertise your business (e.g. hiring a contract writer or marketing specialist). Be sure your advertising is working to help shorten a prospect's purchase decision time, and not to simply generate empty content.

People consume a description of a product before they engage in conversation, much less purchase. As you build, you need to help them understand what you offer, reduce uncertainty about the product's capabilities, and offer customers real reasons to purchase. My advice for shortening a prospect's purchase decision time is to anticipate those needs and:

1. **Write case studies and get testimonials** - Testimonials on a website provide credibility and reduce client risk. Keep detailed case studies of early customers to help you establish routine. Develop a system for bringing on new clients and make the whole process smooth and easy.

2. **Provide a documented process** - This is all to ensure you have an answer when prospects say, "This sounds great. How do we get started?" You might give checklists for site preparation or a chart of available services. The point is to look like you've got matters down to a science. Even if things are still a mess, fake the organization and then update the process once you've learned more about your customers. And if you're creating a pitch deck, I highly recommend including a slide about client onboarding.

3. **Ask for feedback** - This could be a quick message after a Zoom meeting or an email exchange, short survey, or formal questionnaire. Client feedback allows the business to focus on the elements that generate value, and avoids spending money on superfluous add-ons.

Establishing a Niche

After the first couple dozen customers, you work to establish your niche and determine the decision cycle. You need to step back from the details and look at the entire process end-to-end. Initial customers may give you the impression that the sales cycle is three weeks long, but these firms were desperate for a solution and might have found you late in their decision cycle. They might be people who either knew you personally or were referred by a mutual friend or acquaintance. Now you will have to measure the length of the sales cycle because you will be dealing with strangers who exercise due diligence and want a "whole product."

I caution against hiring full-time staff at this stage. It may take a long time to get your revenue up to where you can have an employee and careful planning pays a lot of dividends.

That being said, as you grow and stabilize revenue income, it makes sense to hire some people on a part-time or fractional basis. You may have one or two co-founders with you at the helm, and then you may need some part-time, freelance, and short-term contract hires to help the ship sail smoothly.

Ultimately, the startup is about more than just building yourself a new job. Unless the plan is to be a freelancer, the business needs to be able to scale and grow and that takes a lot more planning than it does seed money.

Scaling

Investing in the team, certainly as you scale above ten employees, is always a good idea. As businesses scale they become subject to all kinds of regulatory oversight and there has to be a plan for consistently delivering value to customers. Many kinds of expenses will be incurred before revenue is collected, so understanding your cash cycle is especially critical. It's important not to make hiring decisions or large capital investments ahead of solid proof of demand.

There are two default extremes that I frequently see based on conversations with founders ready to scale. One is to rely on part-time employees. These entrepreneurs choose to bring in large subcontractors and manage everything as a general contractor and this is okay. But you really can't build a business solely on fractional labor, even if it initially seems like a budget-friendly option. If you plan to take on large projects, there needs to be a system or formal agreement that prevents the subcontractor from—for lack of a better phrase—cutting you out of the deal.

The other extreme is to control everything and have all tasks done by direct employees. This is difficult to manage and scale (and budget). For example, you probably don't need an attorney on staff, but you will need some legal work. And as you secure bigger deals, it becomes harder to control every element. You might not have time to revamp the website or research marketing analytics.

This is when you start to build a company culture, establish internal structures, and shift to hiring specialists. Having a proper onboarding process becomes crucial.

In a startup's early stages, founders must be a jack-of-all-trades-master-of-none, juggling multiple responsibilities and operating within often chaotic business environments. And in order to make things work they hire other generalists who can deal with a range of duties. Now you need those onboarding structures and systems that equip employees for success.

When I first started working at Cisco, my boss handed me a pile of broken monitors and had the new hires figure out how to fix them. Since the company was still in its early days, this turned out to be a fairly good test, because if someone couldn't handle that level of stress they probably wouldn't survive the day-to-day chaos. But again, without an official onboarding process you end up relying on your newest employees to understand their role instead of explaining exactly what the company needs from them.

Closing the Loop

Businesses end up either owning a big chunk of the niche in which they operate, or they might scale up into a new niche. When a company starts to incorporate other products and services, it's back to square one.

When you leave an established niche, you have to go back into the ambiguity and uncertainty of exploration mode: leaving the clarity of execution mode can be painful. We have seen large firms stumble when they leave a well understood market where they are executing smoothly to explore for new opportunities. You may need to regroup with co-founders and form a team for another round of intense research.

Funding Has Many Faces

After calculating expenses needed, and realizing you will require more than you've currently saved, you may Google for venture capital firms in your area and/or create a GoFundMe page.

Venture capitalists might disagree, but other funding options are available depending on where you are in your startup journey:

- Bootstrapping
- Debt Finance
- Equity
- Revenue based financing
- Development partnership
- Don't forget your day job

Bootstrapping

Back in the '80s, I explored the idea of starting a software consulting company. At the time, it cost about $6,000 for an Apple computer (for reference, my business partner bought a new van for this amount) that we could use for software development. This was not a particularly powerful machine but to put things in perspective, my business partner had recently bought a new car for the same price. This one computer would have cost me around three months' salary. We couldn't afford the upfront costs of exploring the idea and had to try something else.

It is now easier to bootstrap startups, with founders using their salary, personal savings, or considerate family members to help pay setup costs. There are free or relatively cheap resources for creating a website, joining a group, and testing some basic software. Calculate what exploring your idea will cost: if it does not entail significant initial expenses, you can bootstrap and worry about investors and bank loans later.

PRO: bootstrapping keeps you focused on what customers are willing to pay for, and therefore what they value. It forces trade-offs early that are focused on customer value. It's also revenue financing and therefore non-dilutive, so if you can make it work, the founders keep a larger slice of equity.

CON: bootstrapping requires you to manage a range of conflicting priorities, from keeping the lights on to pleasing a mix of early customers.

Debt Finance

Debt financing can fund the equipment your business needs, which is pledged against the loan amount if you default. It's using a loan to fund your working capital.

Two of my friends started a Double Rainbow franchise ice-cream store and had to take out a loan to pay for freezers, utensils, ingredients—all the equipment they needed to start selling ice-cream. In total, they had to take out a loan for about $100,000. They borrowed against the equipment and paid the loan off with their profits. That's an option if there is a significant amount of equipment.

PRO: debt financing is a good option for capital intensive startups. It's non-dilutive so if you can service the debt you can keep more of the equity.

CON: if you cannot service the debt you may lose your startup, since debt trumps equity.

Equity

Lenders want to meet current market rates but investors want much more. They want to see a rapidly growing business that can handle a significant return. The money you invest in your business needs to cover salaries, production, and debt and the equity has to be factored into your cash cycle model, with a plan for repayment.

It's important to budget to repay lenders or investors, rather than just meeting an expense obligation. Whether your stakeholders are close friends or venture capitalists, they need to be treated like a business. Money spent on equipment or facilities needs to be able to turn around as profit to repay those debts.

PRO: if you have a business that both merits and requires significant capital, venture capital can provide strong advisors and board members to assist you in growing your firm. A professional investor has a primary objective of getting a return on investment which aligns your interests up to a point.

CON: it's dilutive and can be defocusing if you choose the wrong investors. As you near an exit event such as an acquisition or IPO interests can diverge significantly.

Royalty (or Revenue) Based Financing

There is an alternate venture model that provides royalty-based financing (RBF). These firms make high-interest loans secured by cash flow, rather than investing and taking equity—this is a distinct difference from a bridge loan, which is designed to convert to equity and is part of the traditional VC repertoire. RBF firms' profits are derived from interest on the loan and a share of revenue until the loan is repaid.

They have a different investment thesis but are still trying to pick winners—startups that have reliable revenue streams and have room to grow. They prefer a reliable loan repayment over rapid growth that risks bankruptcy and default. Prominent examples include Royalty Capital, Lighter Capital, and Indie.vc.

PRO: for a business with strong cash flow, this is a viable option to accelerate growth without dilution.

CON: never forget that this is essentially debt; And if things go sideways debt is paid off before any return to the equity holder.

Development Partnership

"I look for a business problem that is so bad, people pay me to solve it and let me keep the software."
Bill Paseman

Early customers agree to act as test beds for development and agree to license the software from you instead of treating it as work-for-hire. Essentially, they agree to pay for some licenses to software or equipment that does not work—yet. For this approach to be viable, you need to bring considerable cost savings, error reduction, or cycle time reduction to an important business process that is not unique to your early customers so that you can amortize the full development cost over many customers.

PRO: this allows you to translate domain expertise and a customer's willingness to act as a test bed to solve a painful problem into non-dilutive revenue. There is a variation where the customer takes equity (typically less than 20%) and acts as a channel for the product.

CON: for the development partnership to work you have to have domain knowledge and some working technology that can form the kernel of a product, and you have to be able to structure the development primarily as the sale of a product, not as a development contract.

Don't Forget Your Day Job

The most overlooked method, however, is to keep your current job and forgo consumption.

This requires buy in and support from your spouse or significant other—and acts as a filter on finding one if you are currently unattached. It's definitely a complicated conversation, but you may be pleasantly surprised. Most entrepreneurs are not very good at hiding their entrepreneurial ambitions.

To forgo consumption means giving up that summer trip to Yellowstone, eating out less often, or sacrificing other enjoyable activities. Accessing savings should also be a mutual decision.

Keeping your current job means not complaining or doing anything that might get you fired. In your mind you can frame your job as temporary to help manage its aggravations and annoyances, but you must not act like a short-timer. It means giving up on career aspirations at your current firm but still meeting the performance requirements. If your current job is intolerable, then find a better one to provide funding for market exploration and product development.

Understanding Customer Values Shortens Time to Revenue

When somebody buys a drill, it's because they want holes in their wall, not because they just want a new drill. Your customer only cares about the results and therefore you need to organize your business to make the value of your product or service obvious to customers.

When entrepreneurs just hope the customer will intuit the product's usability, they have an explanation problem. After the initial sales pitch, buyers need proof of concept. They need to be sure your solution will help them. The sooner they realize your service or product delivers value, the quicker you get to revenue. Ways to provide proof of value include implementation checklists, jumpstart planning, offering a service to debug issues or even pinpoint their

22

operation problems. These are helpful actions that people can pay for and gain trust in your business.

We've seen this with various kinds of bug detection software firms, where they ask their customers to pay for a service first instead of the expensive software tool. The company will charge customers for every defect they find above of a certain complexity. This is simply documenting the labor, being transparent and reducing uncertainty.

Another option is to recommend other solutions when it's appropriate. Do some research, and if the alternative solution is ultimately cheaper and more reliable, you avoid the risk of appearing dishonest. It's better to have that conversation earlier and offer your customer real insight than to sit and pray they never find out about your competition. Later you might follow up and ask how the alternative worked out. For a target set of problems or customers, it's always good to try to understand what the option set is and how it compares to you.

Any information on the target customer base is good information. It prevents entrepreneurs from chasing every opportunity and wasting money on features that don't actually differentiate the product from competitors.

Consider Service First

We always recommend that entrepreneurs start with a service-first approach to shorten time between product iterations. Instead of spending money to build a product and *then* asking for feedback, sell the incomplete solution as a service. This allows you to start making real offers, even if you don't have the necessary funds or equipment for the actual product.

Aside from saving money on development, a service-first approach provides three main advantages:

1. It allows you to configure and adjust a service on the fly, adding manual process steps to aspects not covered by your existing solution (hardware or software).
2. It forces you to focus on the outcome and to determine if it's something the customer wants and is willing to pay for.
3. Because the customer is paying for the outcome, service-first forces you to treat your time as a cost, not valuable or billable in and of itself.

If you find an early adopter who wants the results your technology can deliver, it's much more likely they are willing to pay for *some* results provided as a service than to wait for you to finish the product. This allows you to ask for the order immediately and shortens time to money. Quoting a price and delivering an offer is far more compelling than simply responding to strong interest with, "Sorry, I'll have to get back to you. I'm just doing research right now."

By structuring your initial offering as a service, you can make offers and get feedback on what people want and are willing to pay for and avoid the lag of adding new functionality to meet a revised specification. You also avoid the cost of making the product safe and effective in customers' hands. Since you or a team member will be operating it, you can tolerate some failures and "sharp edges" that would otherwise kill a prospect's desire to use the product.

Commit to Creating Value, Not to a Particular Idea

The two biggest financing mistakes entrepreneurs make are:

1. They don't budget enough time and money for market exploration and customer validation.
2. They don't let go of a bad product idea that's proven to fail.

The challenge to drafting your exploration budget is that it's not clear how long it will take. Probably it will take more time than you would like and will require you to evaluate and tinker with several ideas before you find one that's compelling. This additional time also equates to more money.

Successful individuals and teams take the following three steps to ensure their exploration phase doesn't lead to complete frustration or bankruptcy:

1. They keep their day jobs but set aside some time every week for exploration. In effect, they treat part of their salary as an investment in their next venture.
2. They adjust their lifestyles to allow them to live at a lower spending rate, maybe enlisting the support of their spouse or significant other, and keeping them informed of progress and setbacks.
3. They make a list of good ideas in one to three focus areas where they have experience and demonstrated expertise and they avoid fixating on any one idea simply because it's the only one they have.

You will probably need to explore multiple business ideas, some of which will be mutations of your original idea. The business concept that ultimately succeeds might be remarkably different from your original concept. It's necessary to be ruthless with personal attachment to any one particular concept because it's better to let go of mediocre product ideas that do not inspire customer enthusiasm, much less a willingness to pay.

Getting real feedback on a product can be challenging. You have to like a product idea to invest effort in it, but you cannot assume that prospects will feel the same way. Commit the time to explore its potential in an objective fashion and be ready to Marie Kondo the product idea that does not generate customer attention and interest. It's not uncommon that a lack of interest has nothing to do with the solution you are proposing—you may simply not be addressing a need that a customer considers important.

The best indicator that prospects care about your solution is not an enthusiastic endorsement but constructive criticism. This can either be suggestions for improving your offer or requests for help on a related problem that they consider to be more important.

When a client tells me they need to find "smarter prospects," that's a clear sign they aren't listening objectively. If 30 people were unconvinced that your product could help them, the problem is not with the 30 people. The problem is with either your pitch or your solution's viability. If they tell you how excited they are but don't open their wallets, you have a problem. If they counter with some key improvements that need to be made before they can use the product, pay close attention.

Focus on (and budget for) exploration and validation of an idea rather than the particular idea itself. And make real offers to determine if customers will pay.

Summary

Bottom line: It's much harder to sell a well-subsidized bad idea than a poorly funded good idea.

Regardless of which phase you find yourself in, making offers, maintaining commitments, and consistently delivering value are the cornerstones of a successful, profitable business. While money remains a crucial aspect, intellectual and social capital make up at least two-thirds of that puzzle.

Money can speed up connections and access to resources, but spending money without understanding is wasteful and could hinder development. If you don't listen to your prospects with an open mind, if you fail to calculate the real costs of exploring your idea, or if you fail to devote the necessary amount of time towards building your social capital and intellectual know-how, then the amount of financial capital at your disposal is superfluous.

Key Points to Remember:

- Calculate How Much Money You Need
- Funding Has Many Faces
- Don't Forget Your Day Job
- Understanding Customer Values Shortens Time to Revenue
- Consider Service First
- Commit to Creating Value, Not to a Particular Idea

Email skmurphy@skmurphy.com to receive our free supplemental worksheet on calculating your idea's exploration budget (available as a Google Doc template or Excel file).

Intellectual Capital
A Practical Introduction to the Basics of IP and Cultivating Know-how

"Sweat saves blood, blood saves lives, but brains save both."
Erwin Rommel (attributed)

In entrepreneurial literature there's often an assumption that financial capital is the most important asset. Whether it's a startup, a new product line, or a business unit in an existing business, most writers and pundits focus on the financial capital necessary to launch. This can lead the novice entrepreneur to assume incorrectly that success hinges primarily on money, ignoring the other assets that could contribute to success. Intellectual property and social capital are also necessary. The importance of trust and know-how needs to be emphasized.

When you assume that money is an entrepreneurial panacea, you neglect how intellectual know-how can save money and how social capital can enable you to access future customers. There are trade-offs between these business assets, but no one form of working capital can replace another.

My goal is to provide entrepreneurs with an understanding of traditional IP, practical advice for evaluating individual domain knowledge, and best practices for accumulating relevant know-how.

The Basics of Intellectual Property

IP is the traditional understanding of what constitutes intellectual capital. They include:

- **Trademarks:** A relatively low cost method of protecting the unique names, graphics, and icons associated with your firm and products. These are renewable and are always a good idea for good product names and taglines.

- **Patents**: In certain domains, patents are quite important, but in general, not so much. These can be a source of significant advantage in some industries (e.g. hardware, semiconductors, medical devices), but are less likely to be needed in others (e.g. software). Because they are expensive and can take years, IP attorneys tend to magnify their importance.

- **Copyright:** A default for all of the source code and written materials that you develop that can be secured by marking your source code and content appropriately.

- **Trade secrets**: Non-disclosure forms are necessary for a company's confidential material. It is necessary to identify what you don't want to share with anyone outside the organization and it's a good strategy to limit disclosure to what's strictly needed.

While you need to respect competitors' copyrighted content and trademarks, and also need to be thinking of key names and phrases that might be worth patenting, these legal details are more like housekeeping. It might not be necessary for an early stage startup to spend attorney time on many of the things that large firms pay attorneys to worry about. That being said, it's a good idea to understand some key terms. I've seen firms give away software rights because they didn't understand the legal meaning of certain phrases they copied from a contract found on the internet.

My recommendation for IP management is to focus on key risks and be wary of the limits of legal self-help. If you have a first customer, a clear scope of work or datasheet for the product, and an agreement on value/price, you should find an attorney who would be willing to take an hour or two to prevent basic mistakes. It is definitely worth the fee.

Intellectual Capital Creates Niche Markets

Outside of the classic IP terms and definitions, intellectual capital becomes increasingly difficult to define and quantify. It's sometimes described as domain expertise and know-how, but even that becomes a murky explanation.

I like to define intellectual capital as a solid understanding of your customer's needs within a specific context. It provides your business with a unique, informed perspective—one that may run counter to conventional wisdom—and creates potential for a niche market.

Instead of trying to beat a large firm with resources and funds, operate in a space where you have an informed perspective of the problem. Better still is if you can take advantage of either a significant change in technology or improvements occurring at the intersection of two or three relevant technologies.

One way to illustrate this tech convergence is the transition from the Stone Age to the Bronze Age. First tools were developed based on the mechanical alteration of stone and bone, chipping to make sharp edges. Control of fire then allowed for fire-hardened wooden tools as well as the heat treatment of rocks. Applying fire to clay led to the invention of pottery—going from earthenware, to stoneware, then to porcelain. Then those methods were utilized to smelt copper and when tin was added, the result was bronze alloy, kicking off the Bronze Age.

Long story short: bronze is harder and more durable than either of the constituents, and its manufacturing process was built upon layers of relevant intellectual expertise and know-how. If you can find a way to remix existing elements into a novel form, or build upon existing technologies in a novel but useful way, you can create a powerful new offering and the success of your business will not be solely dependent on financial capital.

How to Assemble Your Existing Knowledge

Organizing and evaluating your intellectual capital is an important early step, especially if you're starting with little money. Developing new insights and know-how means your startup—at least for a while—won't have to compete against well-funded companies.

It can be a daunting task to objectively quantify your knowledge and to determine where you possess measurable expertise and which areas need work. To help smooth this process, I recommend every beginning entrepreneur do the following:

1. Get it out of your head.
2. List your prior failures—and those of others that may be relevant.
3. Decide what's a trade secret.

1. Get it Out of Your Head

> *"Engineers are not superhuman. They make mistakes in their assumptions, in their calculations, in their conclusions. That they make mistakes is forgivable; that they catch them is imperative. Thus it is the essence of modern engineering not only to be able to check one's own work but also to have one's work checked and to be able to check the work of others."*

Henry Petroski in "To Engineer is Human"

Designing a startup is an engineering task. Entrepreneurs need to manage the risk of mistakes and to seek suggestions in the same way that engineers do. They need written down so it can be reviewed in detail. Once they are satisfied they need to solicit critique and listen to suggestions from other team members, advisors, and friends.

First, ideas and thoughts must be transferred to paper or to a computer file to be shared by a team, along with an explanation of what you are doing and why it will work. It's also necessary to be able to transfer this know-how to potential customers in clear language.

31

Your product should target customers and problems that utilize your know-how and domain expertise.

Locate or write down templates, checklists, and diagnostic criteria you used to assess the situation, monitor your actions, and measure the impact.

Also list everywhere you've worked and what was good about it. In particular, systems or techniques that were not only good ideas in the original context, but are likely to be either broadly applicable or portable to other situations. Make a candid assessment of your know-how by listing your past successes and accomplishments. Document the starting situation, the actions you took, and the result or impact. Then weigh which of your past successes, tools, methods, and technologies are most relevant to this new problem you're tackling.

2. List Prior Failures

As loathe as we may be to admit it, the majority of startups fail. Most of your ideas will probably fail, or maybe the way you implement them will fail. But good entrepreneurs learn from their mistakes and each new venture builds on accumulated intellectual capital.

After listing your past successes, make a list of your prior entrepreneurial mistakes and failures and ask everyone on the team to do the same. This graveyard of failed ventures and past mistakes becomes a strategic advantage, allowing you to move through product design and business model iterations more quickly. If you review this list before making significant decisions, you may avoid repeating old mistakes. When you make new mistakes, you'll be uncovering useful new insights rather than "failing."

Next, research what has already been tried and failed to address the same problem you are trying to solve for your target customer. If you are going to introduce something that's "been tried before," be clear in your own mind and at a team level what is different about your new approach and why it will make a difference to your customer.

3. Decide What's a Trade Secret

A trade secret is a recipe that is not obvious and preferably counter to current prevailing wisdom about how to solve a problem. It's part of your "secret sauce" or "unfair advantage," and you are best served by *what* the recipe enables you to make, not the recipe itself.

Early on, you will need to decide what information will not be disclosed outside your team. Typically, a trade secret is a detail of your internal operation that the customer would not be aware of but it is essential to your ability to deliver better results than your competition. Talk about the inputs and outputs to your "black box" but not what's inside.

For software teams, this will be key aspects of your source code that are not easily discoverable from the user interface.

For hardware teams, this may relate to your testing or manufacturing processes.

For service teams, this may be your complete diagnostic or delivery checklists—the customers may see part of them, but only those aspects that are relevant to their situation.

Understanding what's a trade secret also helps translate the technical reasonings behind your product's appeal into easy to understand offers for your customers.

Engineers and developers like to talk about how they have solved a problem, but it's more effective to speak with customers about results and deliverables. If you talk about how you did something, you may accidentally disclose a trade secret. In the worst-case scenario, they might share those secrets with their current vendor or partner because it's easier than switching to you.

How to Accumulate New Knowledge

Intellectual capital is never just *your* intellectual ability or expertise. The loner mentality of bucking tradition, violating the norm, and setting off to explore new fields is a major part of any startup's impetus. An entrepreneur needs a certain amount of that renegade can-do attitude, but also needs to recognize the value of collaboration.

Most expertise is not developed in isolation but is expanded and curated within specific communities of practice. For example, if I'm an excellent chemist, I still need to compare notes with other chemists to improve what I'm doing, or I'll get outperformed by teams who are collaborating and working together. One mad scientist or lone genius is never enough.

If you're trying to create something as an individual, you're probably already part of a community of practice, a group of people who share a concern or a passion and learn how to do it better as they interact regularly. Perhaps you've joined a professional society, a networking meetup group, our Silicon Valley Bootstrappers Breakfast Club, or a university alumni association.

You may be part of a community of practice whose only members are fellow employees of your current company and, won't be able to continue as a member if you leave that company. This is not uncommon for employees of large corporations. A mechanical engineer in a large firm can compare notes with the other mechanical engineers who work there but their accumulated know-how is confined to that one firm's domain. A mechanical engineer who is in a small firm, the only mechanical engineer employed there, or only one of a handful, may find it a challenge to get peer to peer feedback and will need to join another community of practice.

In order to ease transition to startup life, beginning entrepreneurs should join one or more relevant communities of practice that are not limited to a firm's employees.

Summary

Good intellectual capital means being able to make offers built on prior successes that are clear to your customers, which in turn help to establish a niche market.

Build on past success and focus on customers and problems you are not only familiar with, but have tangible expertise. Focus where you have a track record of executing with distinction.

Expert entrepreneurs never try to do something completely new but they leverage collective experience and expertise to their advantage, simultaneously saving money and growing their social networks.

Key Points to Remember:

- The Basics of Intellectual Property
- Intellectual Capital Creates Niche Markets
- How to Assemble Your Existing Knowledge
- How to Accumulate New Knowledge

Email skmurphy@skmurphy.com to receive our free worksheets, designed to help you map previous successful projects and the skills you developed while working on them, and provide your customers and clients with evidence of your demonstrated expertise.

Social Capital

A Practical Introduction to Building Business
Relationships and Leveraging Connections

"You may not have saved a lot of money in your life, but if you have saved a lot of heartaches for other folks, you are a pretty rich man."
Seth Parker

In addition to domain knowledge and an ability to execute, businesses require financial capital to get started. Entrepreneurs rely on both existing trusted business relationships, and their ability to cultivate new ones, as they continue to refine and extend their domain knowledge.

The various formal and ad hoc relationships created while exploring your idea can be just as important as the relationships within a company. These can be a source of trusted feedback and early customers. It's important to maintain good standing in these diverse communities and business networks.

It's about **who you know** as well as **how you know them**. These contacts could come from:

- Family, friends, and acquaintances
- The firm's current suppliers, partners, customers, and advisors
- Co-workers, customers, and suppliers from prior employment
- Alumni: classmates and teachers from high school, college, and university
- Industry, professional, or association memberships
- Permission for contact lists (e.g., mailing lists)

Properly leveraging these relationships enables access to domain experts, introductions to potential cofounders and early employees, and conversations with prospects who may become your early customers.

It's All About Trust

We can't talk about social capital without addressing trust. Trust is an essential element to establishing and maintaining a business relationship, either at a personal or organization level. It's at the core of developing good social capital.

The challenge is to be personable and reliable to contacts and prospects. There can be an urge to cut down on time-consuming tasks, but building trust is an inherently slow process.

Building Trust

The two most important elements of trust in a business setting are: (1) your credibility and (2) your commitment to creating value.

Maintaining good standing is less about personality and likability, and more about authenticity and predictability. Don't start building trust with a "how do I get people to like me?" perspective. Of course, it's a good idea not to antagonize people. Likability plays a large role if you are selling a commodity: if the customer can buy the same product at the same price and delivery terms from many firms, they will buy from a salesperson they like. But in most situations, the attributes and product or service, and the distinct value they offer, make a bigger impact than individual personality.

Borrowing Trust

> "In my early twenties this idea was impressed upon me. I had been doing newspaper work, and as a reporter for a leading daily I was usually received promptly and affably by mayors, bankers, manufacturers, actors, United States Senators, and even presidents of the United States.
>
> I quit my newspaper work and called on a few friends of my newspaper days. I was not insulted when I presented myself, but I

*was not offered cigars with quite the same alacrity as in my
newspaper days.*

*[…] most of us in our working hours are like actors. The power
and dignity and age and good repute of the corporations for which
we work clothes us, and adds to our effectiveness and acceptance by
those whom we serve and who serve us."*

William Feather in "A Jolt" collected in his "The
Business of Life"

Many entrepreneurs get a jolt in their new venture when they
discover that their credibility with strangers, which was once freely
granted by virtue of their employer, must now be earned one
painstaking step at a time. They must make and meet commitments
to prove the value of their word.

If they had fallen into bad habits and were not strict about meeting
their commitments because they could rely on their employer's brand
and reputation as cover, then it would be an even harder climb. A
few years ago, a sales guy who had left a large company to work for a
small firm confessed that when he worked for the established firm,
he had not had to worry about honoring his promises to follow up
and call people back.

The product was in high demand prospects would follow up for him.
Instead of uncovering opportunities and enabling sales, he had
become a speed bump that slowed and deterred conversations. In the
small firm prospects stopped calling and customers disengaged when
they realized he was not reliable. It was a candid and painful
admission. He was not meeting his commitments, not taking care
when making new promises, and not working to diligently follow
through and deliver.

In the same way you don't casually loan strangers our credit cards, or
hand them blank checks, you need to be careful about making

promises and you need to consider carefully who will be allowed to make commitments on behalf of the company.

Keeping Trust

Trust takes time to develop but can be lost quickly and the best way to check is to ask for feedback. Ask customers where they feel you delivered value, and where they feel you could improve. The key is to focus on constructive criticism because if somebody has no complaints, at all they might not care enough to tell you how to improve, or they might be waiting to swap you out. People don't tell you when they start to view you as unreliable or untrustworthy.

Trust also requires mutual respect. Don't say anything behind a customer's back, whether criticism or name-calling, that you would not be willing to say to their face. Sooner or later it will get back to them and will affect their attitude toward you and meanwhile, it will infect your attitude toward them.

If you mislead, lie to, or take advantage of someone, they will find out at some point. From then on, they will be significantly less likely to help you or do business with you. If you or your product fail to meet commitments, customers may decide to do business with someone else. They probably won't mention anything until they've found an alternative. In a sales situation, a prospect may stop responding.

Keeping trust means respecting an appropriate level of respect and confidentiality, if you're helping my business, and consequently you've learned how I operate my service or product, I'm going to assume that you will treat that information as confidential. It would be a terrible move to violate that trust and share in-house secrets.

Use Your Social Capital to Find Prospects

If your connections are outside your target industry or market, at least someone in your social spheres will be relevant to your business.

Everyone knows somebody and your challenge is to help them identify **which** somebody could benefit from your product or service. Talk about your experiences and plainly describe the problem. The more specific the description, the easier it is for people to identify potential customers and the more likely you are to receive suggestions, recommendations, insights, and referrals.

It's tempting to describe things in a general way or to talk about the capabilities that you offer. This inadvertently acts as an IQ test, where you depend on your contact to piece the puzzle together and figure out who is best served by your solution. It's better to be specific about the customer you want to serve and the problem or need you address.

Startup entrepreneurs typically face one of two challenges. They're either developing something novel, trying to fulfill an existing need in a new way or trying to fulfill it in an established way, but perhaps with some differentiation. If you're developing a new solution, you want to focus on who's in pain or is experiencing the problem. People tend to prioritize finding a big market or large audience, when, at least in the beginning, it's better to identify a very specific niche that is in a lot of pain and is willing to pay to have their problem solved. If you're working on improving an existing solution, then the question is not, "Is there a need?" but, "How am I different?" In which case, you want to talk to people that have paid for a similar service or product and interview them.

Otherwise, entrepreneurs end up describing their product or service by saying something like "Anybody could benefit from this." Or they target generic categories by saying, "Small and medium firms would benefit from this." Firstly, aside from maybe the wheel, no invention is going to help **everyone**. Secondly, no one ever defines themselves as a small/medium business person. Instead, they might say that they run a shoe store or own a restaurant.

The goal is to be as specific as possible by describing your business as a solution to a particular problem, not as a list of features. "Contact

CRM," "mobile responsive pages," and "SEO optimization" are not as appealing as "Easily build and market your own website, no software experience necessary." I'm not sure who needs mobile responsive pages, but I do know people looking to quickly create a website for their new startup.

When Talking to Prospects

There are two ways to approach prospects. There's the problem-focused conversation, where you outline the parameters of a good or bad offering. You're talking to people familiar with the problem, who have used similar services or products in the past. Usually the easiest way to approach someone for that conversation is to be candid and say, "Look, I'm thinking about starting a business in X. I wonder if I could get five or ten minutes of your time to talk about your experience with X."

Assume that the majority of people you talk to are introverted. Before a face-to-face meeting (or Zoom call), send an email outlining 3-6 questions and be prepared for the conversation to end in five or ten minutes. If they don't want to talk very much, learn what you can and end the interview. If they're energized and passionate about the topic, still end the conversation after ten minutes, but then follow up with another request to meet. It's much easier to have that quick conversation and then say "I need another 10-15 minutes of your time," than to draw out your initial interaction and completely exhaust their patience.

The second posture is value-focused. The only way to delve into pricing and value questions is to make real offers. You gain much more insight when you ask, "Would you pay x for this?" instead of "How much would you pay for this?" Again, just like with identifying your target customer, you want to be as specific as possible—talking in the abstract just doesn't work here. Your offer needs a deliverable, a turnaround time, and a price. You want your price to be high enough to be credible, but low enough to be a variable. You can always raise your price later depending on feedback, but aware that it is difficult to raise your price with the same individual.

Don't underestimate the marketing potential for multiple sales within an established firm. An entrepreneur who has attended several of our Bootstrapper Breakfasts® recently started a business that melds VR with furniture shopping. His customers can visualize how different desks and tables fit into their house. Due to the coronavirus pandemic, offices have been shut down, and some employees were left without an office space or desk. Google was one of multiple companies to offer a desk renting service to its employees. He capitalized on that, approached Google at a department level, got a foot in the door, and is now benefiting from the company's employees and established reputation.

This is often called a "land and expand" strategy, where entrepreneurs deliver value for a group and move sideways within the firm. You still need to identify your prospect clearly and deliver a concise offer, but it's easier because the next prospect works within the same company.

Use Your Social Capital to Find Cofounders

My bias in businesses I have started has always been to look for cofounders. There are many successful solo founders but I find that it's rare that one person has all the domain knowledge, technical expertise, management experience, and sales skills necessary to get a business off the ground. A team of two or three is often a better bet for viability.

When looking for your team, the cofounder rule of thumb is "shared values, complementary strengths." Many of the serious arguments between cofounders can stem from overlapping strengths. When two people are both strong in the same area, they are often both weak in others. There can be conflict over who's better at something, and common weak spots can be common blind spots. Now everyone's disappointed. The easiest solution is to bring a third person onboard who can complement your skills and expertise.

If you're a business person, you probably have to find a technical person. If you're more of a technical person, you're going to have to find somebody willing to talk about the business and do some sales and marketing. If you find yourself leaning towards ADHD, you may need a partner who has Attention Surplus Disorder.

But these complementary strengths need to exist within shared values.

Determining whether you can share a race car (perhaps a mini-sub is a better metaphor) with someone is complicated and takes time. I recommend talking to several people in parallel, and collaborating on small projects. These projects should act as pressure tests, to see how people react to deadlines and stressful situations. If you haven't already, divide expenses and client payment before agreeing to become a cofounder. You don't marry someone after the first coffee date, right? Go on a real date, then deepen the relationship as events warrant.

Entrepreneurship is a popular topic. Many in Silicon Valley want to be identified as entrepreneurs, but few are willing to leave their jobs and take that risk. Your cofounder needs to be someone who will get in the race car with you, run the course, and accept the possibility of a crash.

Until you find those partners, you need to make progress on your startup alone. Relying on a cofounder to kick-start your business is never an attractive look. Build an Excel model, a WordPress site, attend a Bootstrappers Breakfast—anything to start narrowing down your customer base. And then cobble together something that you can show to attract prospects and potential cofounders.

Tips for Securing Conversations

Calling in favors in the business world is a complex undertaking. It depends on group and cultural norms as well as the depth and duration of your relationship. An engineer, for example, would look at things very differently from a sales rep. To avoid messy confrontations, here are my general guidelines for "spending" social capital.

- **Maintain your network:** If you can, do favors when asked, or say "no" promptly. Your helpfulness will be appreciated and become known to others in the same branch of your network. Keep people up to date on an annual basis about what you are up to and share relevant information about others they may be interested in every 6-12 months. In the long run if all you do is ask for favors, you will burn out friends and associates.

- **Be as specific as possible in your request:** As an example, "I'm working on a team that has recently developed an application that can be used by church choir directors who want to search for music by different criteria, like by the number of different singing roles. If you know someone who is responsible for managing a choir I would appreciate an introduction." Some **unhelpful** phrases people use are:

    1. "Small business." Better would be "a company doing between 2 and 5 million dollars a year in revenue," or "a company with between 10 and 50 employees," or two or three other specific criteria that indicate exactly who you are trying to reach.

    2. "Need our product." Try "has this problem" instead. Phrase the request in terms of needs or problems that a target prospect would know that they have.

    3. "Need a technical person." It's better to list a specific set of skills or accomplishments: for example, "knows Python," "has built websites in WordPress," "is an attorney who has supported other software startups," etc.

- **Contact a few people at a time:** Mass mailing seems more time efficient than contacting people individually by phone or e-mail, but personal requests are more energizing. Mass messaging can lead to so many responses that you're unable to reply quickly: this will damage relationships because they think you're ignoring them.

- **Don't try to run two or more searches at once:** Pick the most important conversation you are trying to have next and focus on that. A request that says, "I am looking for a cofounder like X, and an early adopter customer like Y, and also an investor" is unlikely to generate any action.

- **Close the loop:** Always let people who make a suggestion or an introduction know the outcome. And in case it isn't obvious, be sure to say thanks.

- **Avoid a guilt trip.** Don't start the conversation with "Since I helped you in the past with X, could you help me with Y?" Whether or not you helped someone in the past, assume they don't owe you anything. Instead, say, "Hey, I could really use a favor. Here is specifically what I would like."

- **Understand the opportunity cost to them.** For example, if they own a piece of equipment that is earning them $10,000 a week, asking to borrow it is going to be a huge inconvenience on their part. On the other hand, if you notice that the machine has been largely unused (it's been under a tarp for the past two months, for instance) then loaning it to you for a couple of weeks would be less costly.

- **Take "no" as an answer.** In case this isn't obvious, you need to accept a "no" without getting frustrated. If you someone refuses to give you an introduction, you need to accept their answer graciously. If you end on a positive note, you can come back in a few months and say, "I've made a lot of progress. Can I give you an update on where we are?"

- **When you return a favor, make the benefit match the earlier cost.** Leveraging social capital requires understanding of the imposed cost when someone does you a favor, as well as the value of what they have done for you. You don't have to return a favor immediately and you don't have to ask for one in return soon after someone helps you. But you need to calibrate the cost (to them) and value (compared to your next best option) and make sure things balance out over time.

- **You don't have to wait for them to ask for a favor.** Some people are shy about asking for assistance. If someone did you a solid favor, keep current on their needs and situation and actively offer to assist them in ways that will help move their business forward. Note: giving someone free advice is not returning a favor.

- **Be mindful that you are borrowing credibility when someone makes an introduction.** When you ask a friend for an introduction, it's like borrowing a guest pass. If you behave poorly the third party will hold it against you and also against the person who made the introduction. If things go wrong during your meeting or phone call, and you're rude or impolite, that will negatively affect their attitude towards your friend. This allows you to ask the person who introduced you to check in for unbiased feedback because they know their credibility is on the line.

- **Join a community of entrepreneurs.** In general, you're not going to be directly competitive with most members and will see many opportunities to collaborate.

Most people are looking for help on issues that are important to their company. If you're not working on something they view as a critical issue, it's often better to end the conversation gracefully. People become very interested in what you have to say when they know—and trust—that you can provide value where they need help.

Reputation is Measured in the Context of a Group

It's helpful to have many contacts and business relationships, but it's a mistake to assume that 500 or 1,000 or 4,000 LinkedIn connections equal a tremendous amount of social capital. What transforms these relationships into capital is your understanding of how each person relates to different groups and how they interact, or don't interact, with each other.

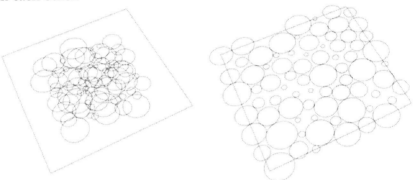

This diagram by Valdis Krebs explains the messy reality of group membership and relationships in a thriving society. The diagram on the left shows that people are members of multiple overlapping intermingled groups, with subgroups and niche communities nestled inside of larger groups and communities. The initial conception, shown on the right, is of clean membership in groups that don't overlap. This can occur if you look for "mutually exclusive, collectively exhaustive" discriminants to separate people into categories, but it doesn't represent how people naturally come to know each other and choose to associate.

Christopher Alexander has explored this complex interaction between people and their membership in groups—referring to the arrangement on the left as a semi-lattice—applying it to city design in his essay "A City is Not a Tree."

After your family and close friends, the smallest group that you are a member of is the small team of individuals you work with daily. That team operates within a company, a self-contained economic unit that provides you with income. If all your meaningful business connections are within that one container, it will be difficult to leave your job. And if you part on less than friendly terms, you might lose access to most or all the people in that container. Then there is the industry group, where multiple companies compete around collectives of customers and suppliers.

Outside your company and industry, there exist three other large groups:

1. **A community of practice**: People engaged in shared learning on topics where they enhance domain expertise by interacting and collaborating with other experts in the same field.
2. **A geographic community**: The people you typically encounter due to shared physical proximity.
3. **An affiliation network**: Voluntary association with others who share values, interests, or goals. For example, an alumni group, a church, a hobby group, or a charity.

Those 4,000 LinkedIn connections are incredibly valuable, but each one represents a different relationship with its own context. Some of your connections might even be competitors. Not every relationship can be leveraged equally and early success in one container might not scale once you leave. Be curious and work to understand where other people's needs and objectives overlap, merge, or operate in tandem with yours.

Summary

You have to network. For a venture to succeed, you have to go out and ask questions. Talk to people who are either proxies for your customer or real prospects. Every fruitful professional relationship has elements of shared success, reciprocity, and predictability.

Be specific when talking to people, whether you're looking for prospects or giving an offer so you can receive specific feedback and critique in return.

Identify a real opportunity before enlisting others. First, focus on proving your idea provides value and then start recruiting cofounders and partners. Once you see that people will pay for your service or product, you can reveal it to others as proof of progress.

Make offers early. Once you think you've got a handle on the problem, start to make offers. While those offers may or may not be accepted, and frequently they are not, they help you iterate faster and narrow your business focus to identify a particular niche. Talking to prospects provides answers and insights.

Individual personality plays a small role. Likeability is a factor, but the real lure is to make commitments carefully and then follow through and deliver.

Key Points to Remember:

- It's All About Trust
- Use Your Social Capital to Find Prospects
- Use Your Social Capital to Find Cofounders
- Tips for Securing Conversations
- Reputation is Measured in the Context of a Group

Email skmurphy@skmurphy.com to receive our free supplemental worksheet, designed to provide you with a working list of past collaborators and set a contact check-in cycle. This gives you an understanding of who best to reach out to for favors, and when to message existing contacts to keep the relationship alive.

Take Stock
Analyzing and Leveraging Your Working Capital

"Every successful person I have heard of has done the best he could with the conditions as he found them, and not waited until next year for better."
Edgar Watson Howe in his book "Country Town Sayings"

Succeeding as an entrepreneur requires a different mindset from working as an employee and technical contributor where you focus on one task at a time. As an entrepreneur and startup founder, you must have a broader understanding of the situation and periodically take stock of all your business assets.

Rather than only looking outward to acquire or develop new forms of capital, entrepreneurs can take advantage of their existing business assets and can rework them to serve operating goals, customer needs, and the emerging demands new prospects may have. Analyzing what financial, intellectual and social capital are valuable, leads to the discovery of new assets, new methods and new abilities.

After investing effort and money to build and improve an asset, it's a good idea to consider new ways to leverage it instead of starting from scratch again. You don't have to reinvent the wheel, especially when the spokes, axle and schematics from the last wheel are still lying around.

When taking stock, these are four critical aspects to think about:

1. What's in your showcase?
2. What is at risk for commoditization or obsolescence?
3. What needs maintenance?
4. What is your competitive advantage?

1. What's in Your Showcase?

Your showcase is the aspect of your offering that attracts inquiries and interest from prospects. The goal is to identify **what your**

customer base is looking for and what assets you need to fulfill that criteria.

It's not necessary to broadcast all of your capabilities. Consider how a car salesman outlines the benefits of a particular automobile. They don't focus on the material that was used in the catalytic converter, but describe the leather upholstery, satellite radio, gas mileage, trunk space and what it would feel like to drive this car.

Another example is which heart-rate monitoring device you want used for the test of your unborn child. How an optically pumped magnetometer functions matters much less than avoiding the need for a lengthy, claustrophobic MRI scan.

In other cases where the technique *is* your product, such as with website development, the "how" can be as much of a selling point as the "why." You know *how* to develop a site with WordPress/Wix/Weebly, *how* to manage it, and *how* to fix any bugs that might creep up. But even then, you are tailoring your pitch to the customer, working with words and tools they are familiar with and omitting irrelevant, in-house information.

Bottom line: most customers simply want to know whether it will meet their needs.

When in Doubt, Look at Customer Requests

The simplest method of identifying what customers are looking for is by listening to customer and client requests and then modify your product or service based on their recommendations.

One example comes from our business cards for SKMurphy, Inc. I handed my business card to someone in 2005 and they asked "Where's your Skype address?" Skype had only been around for a few years, and in my mind it was a way for families to reconnect. I didn't see how it could be applied to a business environment and it didn't occur to me that Skype's popularity would skyrocket.

Originally, all of our clients were located in Silicon Valley, but now we could reach additional people. Distance stopped being a major obstacle. So here's this new technology that has made a significant difference to my life, but I needed a potential client to request a Skype address for me to recognize that and then modify my business cards to accommodate their request.

A technique or resource developed for one purpose can be better marketed in a different way. Maybe a customer "misused" the product and now you've discovered another need to add to your showcase. Or maybe multiple customers made the same request for an additional or different offering. Look at areas where you're getting inquiries and work backwards from what your customers value.

Sometimes the customer is really right and you need to work from their suggestions.

2. What is at Risk for Commoditization or Obsolescence?

"It's always been done this way" is rarely the foundation of good business strategy.

> *"Before desktop publishing, the best way to layout a complicated image for printing was to cut a rubylith. Rubylith is a translucent sheet of thin plastic. A craftsperson would carefully cut the ruby, knowing that the parts it covered would reflect the light when the plate was created. It was difficult and painstaking work.*
>
> *That's all obsolete now. An hour of cutting a ruby is replaced by two clicks in Illustrator. Here's the truth: images cut by hand with a rubylith weren't better. They were simply the best available option."*

> Seth Godin in his blog post "The Truth About Rubylith"

Skills you've mastered with patience and considerable effort, and now have real expertise in, may have become obsolete. In some cases, the new methods and technologies bear little resemblance to the traditional method, but deliver superior results for your customer.

Look at your assets objectively. Listen to what prospects are asking for and learn to let go of the obsolete or commodified aspects of your business and don't hold your business hostage to past decisions.

It's necessary to adapt to changing circumstances and to be aware of your environment and practice by taking stock regularly. The temptation is to always be ahead of every innovation wave but that's just not realistic. You don't want to lag and risk obsolescence of your product or technique.

Our advice: ride the waves. It's hard to predict the future, but, as the old adage goes, change is a constant. Keep an open mind and integrate new technology and processes into your business whenever you can.

3. What Needs Maintenance?

Knowing **when** an asset needs maintenance is both difficult and vital. In terms of expertise/technology, the **bathtub curve** is one method of identifying when something has gone stale. Following the silhouette of a classic bathtub, the graph starts high (signaling lots of initial errors) then swerves down to a flatline (meaning you've mastered the technique and there are virtually no more errors). The amount of errors increases again when an organization rushes to catch up to their new environment and better equipped competitors. If you've been flatlining for a while, there's a real danger of obsolescence and now's the time to take stock and look around.

Additionally, maintenance doesn't have to mean "replace" or "fix." Various elements of your working capital can be "upcycled" or used in a different way.

Money is easy to repurpose. (We're always looking for a bargain.) But leveraging equipment and process capabilities is harder. To determine which assets could be leveraged or repurposed, look at what your business frequently relies upon.

Maintain What You Frequently Use

Create some kind of quarterly review to take stock and assess your working capital. Consider how your assets fit with your business model and ask yourself:

- How has this helped in the last year or two? In the last quarter or two?
- Do you see continued interest?
- How does this fit with where you are trying to go?
- How recently have you used this particular template/building block/piece of content?
- How frequently do you rely on it?

If you are frequently using something, or frequently referring to something, it makes sense to try and squeeze as much utility out of it as possible.

Here's another example from our business: For years I've been tweeting quotes related to startup development and entrepreneurship on our twitter handle @skmurphy. These quotes resonated with entrepreneurs and created additional interest in our company. We have reused them as images in our presentations, postcards for clients and prospects, and even an ebook compilation.

4. Which Business Assets Contribute to Your Competitive Advantage?

The goal is to be easy to discover but hard to copy. Discoverability means that you are constantly showcasing all the solutions you offer. Copiability refers to the creation of your particular niche and customer base as a means of eliminating competition.

The drive to narrow your niche could come directly from your customers. They might ask for a cheaper version of an existing product or service or they may be unhappy with the way you're operating compared to other businesses. Or maybe you're trying to sell something that your clientele has never asked about. In which case, be careful to not build up business assets for a Swiss army knife when all your customer wants is a pair of scissors. If all they want is scissors, and you can make scissors really well, sell the product that's easier to manufacture, maintain, and pitch.

Be very clear about who your organization is serving and focus on developing assets that will satisfy *your* prospects, and not on assets that will simply "round things out."

Social Capital is Different

Unlike your standard business assets and working capital, accumulating expertise and developing trust takes a long time. So once you've built these solid relationships, work to maintain and leverage them rather than starting from zero all over again.

Maintaining shared trust and mutual connection requires a proactive, personalized approach. Setting a "check-in cycle" for contacts is highly recommended. Customers, partners, suppliers and manufacturers should be regularly contacted so that you are constantly aware of what is expected of your organization and what you can realistically deliver. People you have shared a success story with, who should be part of your LinkedIn network, can be contacted at least on a yearly basis.

Reconnecting can be triggered by something you have learned that you want to share because you believe it will be of benefit to them. The less widely known something is and the more you connect the dots to how you believe it may affect their business, the more valuable it is. It's fine to include a brief "what I have been up to" or to use recent good news as a reason reach out, but your description must be brief and to the point—everyone is busy—and should illustrate the unique methodologies and services you offer.

Proactively share *your* meaningful personal insights and don't default to the common wisdom message of the month. Provide thought leadership by discerning important events and trends at work in the present, predict their likely effects, and offer perspective and actionable advice in time to have an impact. This definitely requires more effort than the odd spam message, but that's what makes it all the more effective.

Making introductions is another method for staying on someone's radar, but your introductions must be personalized and include the reasons why you believe that parties are likely to benefit from a conversation.

Maybe you've operated in one industry, worked with a set of people, pooled your knowledge together, but now they've gone to another company and you're building a startup. Whether or not everyone is still working within the same industry, it helps to reach out to people with whom you've shared a success story and ask if there is some way their capabilities could work in your firm/industry. Start sifting through contacts and think in terms of "calling in favors." Their capabilities might no longer fit with your goals, but they might introduce a new connection.

Summary

There is no universal list of business assets that applies to every product and every company. I encourage you to take stock periodically, determine which assets attract customers, differentiate your offering from competitive alternatives, and deliver value.

Changes in customer needs, the technology landscape, the economy, and the competitive arena may have made some assets obsolete and left others in serious need of renewal. Consider how you might repurpose or redeploy assets to efforts that may yield more revenue, more profit, and higher customer satisfaction.

Key Points to Remember:

- What's in Your Showcase?
- What is at Risk for Commoditization or Obsolescence?
- What Needs Maintenance?
- Which Business Assets Contribute to Your Competitive Advantage?
- Social Capital is Different

Plan Your Startup

Assembling All Three Forms of Capital to Launch
Your Idea

"Even with a dull axe, you can blaze a trail."
Robert Powers

I frequently use the phrase "entrepreneurial journey" when I talk with
and consult first-time bootstrappers and startup founders. But
looking through my explanations, I've come to realize that the
"journey" metaphor is not as useful or accurate as I had thought. It's
more about constructing an ecosystem of relationships—almost an
organic entity—rather than racing towards an arbitrary finish line.

Instead of paving a path for others to journey across, I want to
provide entrepreneurs, both first-time and repeat offenders, with the
tools necessary to survey and cut their own paths (even with a dull
axe).

And while the final course may be different for each entrepreneur
and business, every startup begins with these ten steps.

1. Understand the Legal Constraints

Beware of Overlap Between Current or Former
Employers and Your Startup

Under California law, what individuals do on their own time and with
their own materials or resources, is their own property. Other states
have different laws, so I urge entrepreneurs to familiarize themselves
with those legal constraints and maintain a clear separation between
company property and equipment used for a new venture. My rule of
thumb: only take what's in your head.

If possible, avoid competing with your current employer. Start something that is complementary, or that only competes with a small aspect of the company's products or services. Consider targeting your old firm's setup requirements—what they need to get started—or focus on opportunities they have enabled after their product or service is sold and delivered. In general, it's usually safer to strike out in a new direction and avoid the mess of ethical and potential legal problems altogether.

If you are unemployed, the good news is you can talk to people at any time and are not limited by regular working hours. It's still not a good idea to compete directly with your former employer, especially if you have not parted on friendly terms. Previous contacts from that former employer will be more likely to help if your venture is not in direct competition with their livelihood.

2. Budget For Your Idea

Successful teams often have to explore several ideas before they find a winner and even then it can take a while for it to start generating revenue, much less profit. Set a time limit to explore an idea, anticipating that you may need to examine several ideas before you find a winner.

Even if you managed to conjure the perfect solution (which alas is more unlikely than either of us would like), that idea may not turn a profit for at least six months to a year, and sometimes longer. This is especially the case if you measure profit not only as covering the additional expenses that the startup is incurring but also replacing your current salary (or at least funding a minimal lifestyle while you focus primarily on your startup).

Calculate Your Living Expenses

Whether you are working part-time or full-time, or you are interviewing for work, you need to figure out your living expenses. The advantage of making this runway calculation is that it forces you to set some time limits, which is especially important if some of your expenses are subsidized by a significant other, understanding spouse, or supportive relative.

Make a list of what you need to support your life (e.g., rent, utilities, groceries, clothing, transportation, entertainment) and then what you will need for that to be sustainable for at least 1-2 years. Using one to two-year time frames force you to consider what will be involved in living more simply long enough to make sure that your idea is viable.

Remember: this is not planning for a camping trip; this is preparing for a move to the wilderness.

Calculate Your Exploration Expenses

When considering how much it will cost to explore your idea, look at which research/experimentation methods will get you an answer quickly and reliably, and which will also help reduce risk or uncertainty in your potential business. Calculate not only how much money you will require, but how much intellectual capital (expertise you can leverage or may need to develop), social capital (trusted connections who can advise and open doors), and time will be needed.

Broadly there are two categories of risk you need to account for:

1. Can you make your production function correctly and is it feasible?
2. Is this something that people will pay for?

These two combine to yield a third risk: if the value that your product provides—as measured by what people are willing to pay for it—is less than what it costs to make, sell, and service, then you won't be profitable.

The exploration phase is essentially a series of small experiments starting with hypotheses on who your target customer is, a particular problem they have, and a solution you can offer that they are willing to pay for. You then adjust one or more of these based on feedback and critique. You're not searching for statistical validity, you're just trying to determine your business's direction.

The goal is not to budget for a completed product, but to budget for a demo or example that verifies that you are working on an important problem for a customer—meaning one they are willing to spend money on—and communicates your solution and its benefits clearly. This could be a scale model, a wireframe, a success story, or even a piece of paper. Go ugly early, focus on the bare minimum needed to deliver your service, and see what triggers a response.

For example, if I wanted to test a new software idea, I would keep the user interface very simple. I would postpone writing 90% of the error checking in order to get a testable model out quicker. Once I was confident there was strong interest and a willingness to pay, *then* I would update the software and complete other tasks I deferred.

The combination of your living expenses and your exploration budget defines the financial capital bootstrappers will need. This doesn't have to be a lump sum. If you have a job or a freelance gig, you can pay as you go as long as your costs don't exceed your income.

Manage the Work-Work Balance

The work-work balance is the need to earn money while you are engaged in getting your startup off the ground. Often this means having to freelance or continue your day job much longer than you would like in order to fund your market exploration, customer discovery, and early sales efforts. Avoid the very real temptation to go all in on the pursuit of one visionary idea, until you have paying customers and a debugged process for finding, closing, and keeping new customers.

Managing the work/work balance means satisfactory performance at a job or series of freelance gigs that pay the bills. You need to let go of the "above and beyond" work necessary to advance in a career to give yourself time and energy to build your own firm. It's hard, but despite how you may feel, it's not harder than managing the mix of interrupts and conflicting goals you will need to navigate when you go full time on your own.

3. Be Smart and Frugal, Not Short-Sighted and Cheap

Throughout the exploration phase cut corners and curb costs where you can in order to iterate rapidly. Eventually you will need to spend money. The challenge is to determine when a low-cost approach is acceptable and when it will make you appear cheap (and therefore low quality), short-sighted, or untrustworthy.

Simulations and models can help you save prototyping expenses when done correctly. Ray Kroc recounts the following example of simulating an imaginary business in his book *Grinding it Out.*

> *"An equally unusual thing happened in 1953 when the McDonalds were designing their "golden arches" building. They wanted to lay it out in the most efficient way possible, placing windows and equipment so that each crew member's job could be done with a minimum number of steps. Mac and Dick had a tennis court behind their house, and they got Art Bender and a couple of other operations people up there to draw out the whole floor plan with chalk, actual size, like a giant hopscotch. It must have looked funny as hell–these grown men pacing about and going through the motions of preparing hamburgers, french fries, and milkshakes. Anyhow, they got it all drawn, just so, and the architect was to come up the next day and copy the layout to scale for his plans."*

Ray Kroc in his book "Grinding it Out"

Be smart about testing products and services, avoid engaging in a false economy, and spend money on what works. To a certain extent, there are equipment and facilities to borrow, favors to call in, and domain expertise to leverage to cut initial costs. But if you try to do everything for "free," things will fall apart. You will end up owing too many people too many favors, and exhausting whatever reservoir of goodwill you started with.

An Example from Genentech's Founding

Here is another example recounted from "Something Ventured" about the founding of Genentech. Tom Perkins is the Perkins in Kleiner-Perkins and Herb Boyer is one of the founders:

> **Tom Perkins:** They wanted to raise $3M to build a factory and hire people to see if it would work. But underlying it all was the tremendous risk factor of "would it be possible?" It was pure research. Everybody knows that venture capital should never openly fund pure research. ***My idea in everything has been to address the risk up front and to get rid of the risk as fast as you possibly can.***
> **Herb Boyer**: Bob and I were very naive about how we were going to do it.
> **Tom Perkins**: We changed the business plan. I persuaded them to do it a different way, to subcontract the experiment to two different institutions.
> **Narrator**: By subcontracting, Tom Perkins eliminated the need to buy equipment, build a lab and hire staff. The estimated $3M startup costs were reduced to $250,000. Kleiner-Perkins put up the money and Genentech was in business.

Rather than spend time and money on a "maybe", Genentech leased a lab for a year to figure out if their idea was technically feasible and **then** set about producing it the right way.

Your exploration needs to cover feasibility, desirability, and profitability.

Investors are not art patrons, they are not interested in something beautiful. They want you to create a business that will repay their investment. As an entrepreneur, you need to adopt this same mindset especially since you are making an investment in yourself and you want that investment will be repaid. You need to determine how the results of your efforts are going to connect to revenue and profit.

The three key goals of the exploration phase are to make sure you can create something:

1. that works (feasible)
2. that people want (desirable) and will pay for
3. at a profit (viable)

Focus For Effect: Sell What You Have

There comes a point when you need to focus and narrow your exploration to a particular set of customers who have very similar needs—needs that can be addressed by a common feature set. A key challenge is determining who will be guided by your early customers' purchase decision.

If a new prospect is not swayed by your results with previous customers beware of adding too many new features in order to address their needs. If the majority of your current feature set does not add value for a new prospect, then embarking upon a significant expansion of your product for one deal is probably a bad idea compared to trying to sell what you have to other prospects.

For entrepreneurs who have a freelance development or consulting background this can be a particular challenge, as they have been successful historically by chasing contract development opportunities. If you find yourself adding major new features to secure each new customer, you lack the focus needed to develop a successful product.

To summarize, focus on a single set of features or services to avoid spending money and time chasing an endless stream of tangent opportunities.

4. Assemble Your Know-How

Entrepreneurs face a choice of either contending with well-funded competitors or exploring a highly uncertain market. One way of reducing uncertainty is with direct knowledge of the market (which may not be widely available), or to leverage expertise with a new tool or technology that is not yet widely understood.

We've already talked about evaluating your knowledge base and joining relevant communities of practice in order to help build your intellectual capital and domain expertise.

Another method is by listening to customers. Sometimes people coming from a business background can quickly intuit a solution based on a customer problem. They see a need and add product capabilities to match. Salespeople who interact directly with customers, hear where the product is failing and base an idea on a new service or "Version 2.0" of the existing product.

Be conscious of where you are looking because big companies can draw on seemingly limitless resources. They can access their team's knowledge, their manufacturers' knowledge, and their customers' insights.

In the beginning, when the possibilities are still unclear, larger competitors might be happy to sit back, either because they don't believe that the market exists or don't believe that it will be big enough to merit their investment. They can't afford to chase the "small" million-dollar opportunities. But unlike big companies, entrepreneurs are not bound to capital hurdle rates and can absorb the affordable loss of chasing after markets that become significant. Entrepreneurs are initially fighting the status quo of existing solutions, but need to be on guard for a large competitor to realizing there's a significant market. It will mean new and serious competition.

Taking stock of what you know and identifying what is not widely appreciated or (even better) runs counter to conventional wisdom, will help identify where you can gain an edge over larger competitors. If you are competing against small and equally nimble and knowledgeable competitors, you will have to outperform them.

Narrow Your Research Focus and Be Objective

If you are excited about your startup's technology or field of study and enjoy learning about it, but have only worked on real projects outside of that domain, the venture might be more of a hobby or research interest.

It's good to have an active mind and curiosity on a variety of subjects, but you can't spend all your time on abstract and theoretical subjects. At some point you have to start making offers, reaching out to future prospects, and narrowing your customer niche.

Secondly, be objective as you assemble your know-how and avoid what I like to call the illusion of omnicompetence—the "I don't know much about this field, but it can't be that hard" train of thought. **All expertise has limits.** You may have a low opinion of people who work in a particular field and believe they are not as intelligent or skilled as you are. But that does not mean that they have not developed competencies and solved problems that you may not even be aware of.

The teams that are most likely to succeed combine people with current experience in the relevant domains with one or two who are bringing proven experience from a seemingly unrelated field. This gives the team to question existing practices--they have to explain to the newcomer why things are done a certain way. And it allows them to import proven practices from other industries or domains that prove surprisingly relevant to long standing problems in the target niche.

5. Assemble Your Team

Every startup team needs experts in development and sales. The founders must appreciate both.

Let me use an estuary as a model. An estuary is a body of water or wetlands where freshwater lakes and rivers flow into a salty ocean. Depending on the time of year, that transitional area becomes either more salty or more fresh. For our purposes, the ocean is the production operation for the client you're trying to serve. The freshwater river represents your R&D and innovation centers. And the estuary is how you link the two areas of your business.

A bootstrapping startup must balance attracting, closing, and servicing customers with ongoing product and service improvements. You need to increase the value and differentiation of your offering while selling the current product and servicing existing customers. In the estuary model, the level of innovation corresponds to the salinity of the water. The team members that live in the technology transfer area between development and support need to be comfortable working with people who operate at both ends of the process. They need to convey the benefits of new features to customers and prospects, and they also need to explain to development what customers and prospects feel is missing or needs improvement. Normally, founders spend most of their time neither completely customer-facing, nor completely focused on development.

It is crucial to employ real-time systems for shared planning, and manage the sales pipeline and development roadmap in parallel. Having world-class experts is great, but versatility and cooperation are imperative.

There is a temptation to try and hire a dedicated sales person early, but if you cannot make them a founder then you should learn how to sell your product *before* hiring them. If you—as a founder—cannot sell your product, no one will be able to do it for you.

We consult mainly engineers and scientists and the first thing we tell them is that they have to learn how to sell. If you don't know how to sell your idea, then you must be willing to learn or to add a cofounder who can.

At a minimum, you're going to need two types of people: an Inside Person, who can keep operations moving forward in terms of development, and an Outside Person, who's willing to go out and talk to people. At a bare minimum, both have to communicate and work together effectively. If you are an Inside person, either adopt and embody an Outside mindset or find someone else to join the venture who can. Not everyone is going to be a full-time member, a small startup doesn't need a full-time webmaster or attorney and in the age of outsourced servers and virtual meetings, you don't even need a full-time office building.

However, finding the right people is essential and requires a clear understanding of the skills, experience, and values they will need to contribute to the team.

It's rare that strangers can immediately form a viable team. By definition, a bad hire was a good interviewer and an interview cannot duplicate the stress of working to meet a deadline in a small team.

We recommend first paying people to work with you on a small joint project: get acquainted in a more realistic environment. The end of the project then acts as a natural and graceful exit point, for you and for them, enabling you to maintain goodwill in any shared communities that you both operate in.

Too often, founders and early-stage teams do the equivalent of bringing an engagement ring to the coffee date. It's important to allow everyone to understand what they are signing up for and allow a painless exit for all parties if things don't work out.

Keep in mind that it's important that your fellow team members share your sense of mission. Entrepreneurship has been romanticized into Silicon Valley's version of the Wild West. It reeks of adventure and reward. But in actuality, it's a harsh, unforgiving landscape. It takes a certain amount of insanity to leave civilization for the lawless wilderness, and not many people are crazy enough. So if you can hold a regular job, you probably should. And it's paramount that you and your team are not working on an idea because "startups are cool," but because you all believe in the mission.

There's a quote by playwright George Bernard Shaw that reads, "The reasonable man adapts himself to the world: the unreasonable one persists in trying to adapt the world to himself. Therefore all progress depends on the unreasonable man."

I have taken the entrepreneurial lifestyle to heart since I first started driving. I spent time in larger firms but realized I was better suited to dealing with entrepreneurs' psychological problems than the political challenges inherent in the enterprise. I want to assure you that Shaw is correct: you need the crazy, unreasonable people to drive innovation. However, your team of "unreasonable" people still need to be able to compromise, disagree-but-support, and move forward.

To recap: A good team consists of Outside people, Inside people, mavericks, developers, go-betweens, previous coworkers, industry experts, cowboys, and at least one very lucky person.

6. Talk to Prospects

You've budgeted for a segue into the startup world. You've developed a list of ideas and opportunities to explore. You've assembled a team that can work together. The next step is to start making offers against one or more of those opportunities and begin the learning process. (Though ideally, you've been talking to potential prospects from day one.)

When creating a new product/business, we tend to focus on the in-house details: what are we doing and what do we need. But say my headlights break and I take my car to the mechanic. I don't want to know from where the parts are sourced or what tools will be used. I just want to know whether it can be fixed, how long it will take, and how much I have to pay. Instead of boring or confusing the customer with a description of **how** you will solve their problem, talk about the results your product delivers. Describe the solution and not the process.

A strong, negative reaction is better than a lukewarm reception. If you talk to someone about this particular problem and their response is, "that's nice," or "it's not really a problem for me," then you're not gathering evidence that will lead to useful insights. You want a stronger reaction, positive or negative. If people who fit your target customer definition aren't interested in discussing the problem, or giving feedback, or even criticizing your idea, then it's back to the drawing board.

Your core objective in talking to prospects is not gaining their approval, it's clarifying the problem you're trying to solve. Desperation is a good indication that there's a real need for your idea.

If I had a leaky pipe, for example, that was preventing me from showering or even flushing my toilet, then I would be pretty desperate for a solution. If a plumber will take days to come, I might settle for wrapping the damaged pipe in duct tape so I can at least shower. It may only hold until the plumber comes but at least it's **something**. The point is, people that are in pain accept partial solutions because they simply want the situation to improve. Duct Tape would improve things for a little while at least.

Revisit where you developed your original belief and determine what alternatives you are making obsolete. Figure out what your prospects will stop doing if they pay for your offering. Write about the problem from a prospect's perspective and see if you get readers and identify prospects who are in enough pain to be willing to take a chance on an incomplete or partial solution (your startup's current offering is certainly incomplete compared to where you will be in a year).

Entrepreneurs can get caught in a "perfection cycle" mindset, where prospects claim that they need the product to be perfect and meet all their needs before taking action. But what are their alternatives? If a prospect is willing to live with an alternative until yours is perfect, they are not a real prospect and their attitude does not mean your product idea is not viable.

There's a balancing act here. Sometimes your solution is completely inadequate, but sometimes you don't have enough of your product or service available to convince your audience and differentiating between the two is no easy task.

Warning: Don't Assume Everything is a Nail

One of the most common entrepreneurial failings is to pick up a hammer and, at that instant, assume everything else is a nail. I meet entrepreneurs all the time who are gripped by their new product, convinced that it's the best thing ever and everyone will want to use it. Sadly, I have to tell them to ignore their idea's shiny, mesmerizing hold and focus ruthlessly on where it brings customers value.

Edison's description for the phonograph, for instance, originally included a myriad of uses. He envisioned his product being used for audiobooks, dictating letters, recording family histories, and even as an audible clock. However, the phonograph's number one selling point was that it could play music.

Inventors may see countless possibilities for their product, but only a few will get traction in the beginning and lead to revenue. The challenge is to make offers and listen carefully to where customers see a clear benefit that's distinct from the other alternatives available to them.

7. Know When to Stop Talking to Prospects

As a rule of thumb, talk to 20-30 people. If those 30 people can't relate to the problem, or are not interested in your solution, that doesn't necessarily mean you have a bad idea. You may not be working on a real problem, but there also might be some selection bias inadvertently excluding the real prospects.

A couple of years ago, we were working with a client who wanted to explore the demand for a chip design tool. They wanted to solve an issue referred to as Clock Domain Crossing, where you have multiple clock domains on a single chip. The founders had worked at a company where they had managed to solve that problem, and were now looking to offer the solution to other companies. We talked to at least 20 chip design engineers and unfortunately none of them could relate.

We persevered because we knew the team had come from an environment where this was definitely a real issue and ended up at a specialty conference for chip designers. This time, when we asked if people were facing Clock Domain Crossing issues, about a dozen people raised their hands. We had found our prospects.

Customer research and customer discovery are never really finished. You can talk to a hundred people, and have several of them buy, before you find your true customer base. Or you may shift to another problem after talking to 20 prospects. But whether you choose to pivot or persevere, you will need to continually check the viability of your service or product and grow your understanding of its market value. The only way that you prove desirability is by getting paying customers.

Too many startups fail because they assume that a promise to pay for a service in the future is the same as customers actually buying. You can't rely on surveys; you have to make a real offer and get paid, over and over again.

8. Be Mindful of Cash Flow

While acquiring early customers and building your venture, there are two major cash flow concerns to keep in mind:

1. not calculating payment delays and
2. not considering opportunity costs.

Payment Delays

Sending out bills does not equate to having cash in the bank. Depending on your client, it may be 60 to 90 days before you're paid and that lag time needs to be factored into your revenue calculations and payment model. You may have an order for $100,000 of product from somebody, but certain features need to be added before you can collect the final payment. Even with that $100,000 contract in hand, a startup could fold because there is not enough money to finish development and deliver. Instead of one big payment, I always suggest breaking it up into phases. That way, the first phase's payment can go back as an investment on the next phase.

Another way to help cut payment delays is to offer discounts and incentives for faster payment. One common discount is 1.5% to 2% for payment within ten days of the invoice date.

On the other side of that equation, be sure to pay your subcontractors and suppliers on time. Smaller firms don't have the prestige of corporate giants, and if you don't pay promptly, businesses will just walk away. Small payment miscalculations or delays serve to erode trust in your company.

One last bit of advice on dealing with payment delays -- prioritize your bills. Before you even have the money, there should be a plan in place for where it should go.

Lost Opportunity Costs

Like I mentioned above: Bigger deals aren't necessarily better. The bigger the deal, the more the risk. Startups are liable to invest more resources in anticipation of a big deal but if (for whatever reason) it doesn't go through, and the customer decides not to pay, that's wasted time and effort.

Even if the contract pans out, other customers and other opportunities might have been put in jeopardy. Your team can't work 24/7. So make sure that people are working on what will generate value and lead to revenue.

9. Learn from Failure

As loathe as we may be to admit it, failure is inevitable. And the benefits of acquiring the ability to learn from failure are too often overlooked.

Allow me a quick sidebar: Dr. Charles Townes developed the concept of the laser and won the Nobel Prize in 1964. He continued to make fundamental innovations in various branches of astrophysics for another two decades. Townes described two kinds of feedback he encountered when exploring concepts for new instruments. Some people would say, "That'll never work." He learned to ignore this answer. Other people would say, "That's very interesting, but previous inventors were never able to get past this problem or this constraint." Townes paid close attention to the specific, possible defects in his approach.

He ignored the generic cries of futility while incorporating the informed skepticism into his approach. So should we all.

Another metaphor: if you watch an infant learning to walk, you will see them fall constantly. And after every stumble, they get up and try again. As adults, we tend to stop after the first tumble or two. I don't mean to suggest that entrepreneurs embrace failure and leap towards misguided ventures. Failure sucks. But as a bootstrapper, you have to be willing to experiment with lots of different ideas and methods, especially if you're developing something in a relatively new field.

The secret to the infant's success is that they weigh very little and don't fall very far at all. You need to adopt this same approach, crafting safe-to-fail experiments, and only risking losses you can afford in your market exploration efforts.

The experienced entrepreneur knows how to harness failures productively, and prefers making new mistakes to repeating old ones. They also learn from others' mistakes, knowing that they can learn as much in the library or in conversation with other experts as they can in their own lab. This allows them to explore ideas that have failed previously and solve them by bringing in new insights or new technologies.

10. Join a Mastermind Group

Perhaps the most underrated step of all is joining a mastermind group. Coined in 1925 by author Napoleon Hill, a mastermind group is essentially peer-to-peer mentoring. As you develop and grow your business, you'll gain new insights and expertise but your startup knowledge is never limited to just *your* knowledge. There's no need to solve every problem alone.

I highly recommend joining a group of like-minded entrepreneurs, preferably a mix of novice and experienced members, in order to obtain:

- Supportive feedback on complex business issues.
- Accountability on critical risk-reducing issues that really move your business forward.
- Useful advice from experienced founders and mentors.
- Additional resources.
- A greater understanding of potential pitfalls and solutions.

Our SKMurphy Mastermind Group meets twice a month for about two hours. Our members are entrepreneurs and founders of early stage startups, committed to growing their business ventures from the inside-out.

I encourage you to attend at least one meeting. Whichever group you join, peer discussions often yield different perspectives on current challenges, and encouragement to meet future goals.

And No, It Never Gets Easy.

As soon as you start to be successful, people take notice. They look for ways to do the same thing cheaper, or faster, or better in a different way. Take the TomTom GPS, for example. They had this great piece of hardware for locating stuff, and it was super successful. They never anticipated that Apple would add the same capability to iPhones and take away a lot of their business. TomTom had all the expertise and manufacturing capabilities, and then Apple comes out of left field and approaches the same problem in a completely different way.

Sometimes the person who's first doesn't win. Sometimes seventh place wins. Sometimes cheaper wins, sometimes better wins, sometimes different wins. There is no real equilibrium point where you've achieved success, and life is easy. You're continually building a knowledge base, and cultivating an ecosystem of relationships with partners and customers. That's why it's crucial to keep re-examining existing assets, reconnecting with people, and continuously reviewing your product's feasibility, desirability, and profitability.

Final Thoughts

Your business is built atop financial, intellectual, and social capital. The understanding of how those assets operate, how to cultivate them, and how to leverage them is at the core of every successful business.

Financial capital gets most of the ink in the startup trade press—certainly what's written or sponsored by venture capitalists—but it in my experience it ranks about fourth in importance below the following:

- **Team Morale** - the social capital of your team. If people are not happy and energized by working together, then it will be hard to persevere.
- **Know-How** - especially practical knowledge of how to solve a category of problems, in particular know-how that is not widely known or appreciated, or even counter to current conventional wisdom.
- **Reputation and Trust** - the social capital external to your team. Even if you are the smartest team on the planet, if prospects won't trust you and your customers won't vouch for you, you will not prosper.

Financial capital is an important asset in terms of developing a viable business. But your know-how, experience, and relationships with teams, customers, and partners are more important.

If you are just starting out, it's almost certain that you will need to explore multiple adjacent business ideas before finding one that resonates with and provides value for your customers. Don't believe the fantastical origin stories of established firms. I refer to the ones that start with a single flash of insight, leading to a smooth clean thrust of the market and ending in massive (or at least modest) success. At the end of the day, being able to let go of a bad idea in favor of a better one is as important as persevering with a good one.

And as you explore a multitude of ideas or idea variations, remember that creating a startup is less like a sprint than a marathon. This means that you need to maintain your customer relationships, renew your know-how in light of new technical developments and scientific insights, and continue to reach out non-customers, because it's in the latter group that new entrants will start with before they come to your core market(s).

You can make a profit once you've solved the unknowns and reduced uncertainties around your service or product model. And once you're ready, there are many books, blogs, podcasts, and webinars devoted to funding and profit. After you've found your first niche I think the challenges facing a startup mirror the growth of a settlement into a village and then into a town. Someday your startup may even become a big city.

Even if you are already established and successful in one or more markets you will still face an ongoing stream of new competitors and potential encroachment by larger and more established firms who want to add your market to their list of profit sanctuaries.

And no, it never gets any easier.

About the Author

Sean Murphy has worked in a variety of roles over the last forty years: as a software engineer, engineering manager, project manager, in business development, product marketing, and customer support. Companies he has worked directly for include Cisco Systems, 3Com, AMD, MMC Networks, and VLSI Technology.

Mr. Murphy has experience working for startups in cofounder and early employee roles as well as in management positions in large companies. He has been on both sides of the table: selling new technology developed by startups to large firms and acquiring it from startups and shepherding its adoption in large firms. He has often acted as a change agent inside of larger firms, helping to foster significant process improvements in engineering, support, and marketing functions. These changes often relied on the integration of outside technologies with internally developed capabilities, where the combination enabled significant improvements in the value of existing products or services to customers.

He has a BS in Mathematical Sciences and an MS in Engineering-Economic Systems from Stanford.

In 2003 he formed SKMurphy, Inc. to consult early stage startups, helping other entrepreneurs and bootstrappers to generate leads and close deals. In addition to providing advisory and consulting services, SKMurphy offers workshops and facilitates mastermind (peer to peer advisory) groups.

In October of 2006 he started the Bootstrapper Breakfasts® as a service to bootstrappers in Silicon Valley. These are roundtable discussions where entrepreneurs can compare notes and gain new perspectives on the challenges of growing their businesses.

In 2006 he started blogging at www.skmurphy.com/blog and has published over 1,900 blog posts totaling about 1.5 million words as of mid-October, 2021. Portions of this book started out as blog posts from his SKMurphy blog.

The material in this book is based on his direct experience working for companies large and small as both a technology developer and as an internal system integrator for engineering teams, negotiating software license deals for tools that were incorporated into internal service processes.

This book is the first in a multi-volume series on building successful startups, please contact skmurphy@skmurphy.com if you have topics you would like to see addressed in a future volume.

Made in the USA
Columbia, SC
12 June 2024

36503658R00046